Passing the Baton

Launching Your Christian Life Coaching Practice

Dr. Stan DeKoven

Passing the Baton

Launching Your Christian Life Coaching Practice
Dr. Stan DeKoven

Copyright © 2018 by Stan DeKoven

ISBN 978-1-61529-208-0

For information on reordering, please contact:

Vision Publishing
P.O. Box 1680
Ramona, CA 92065
(760) 789-4700
www.booksbyvision.org

Table of Contents

Foreword

A few years ago, I was a full time Marriage and Family counselor with a substantial practice. Counseling is important for those in need of working through life issues. It is significant, that approximately 10% of men and women in local churches need some intensive counseling at any given time and often this 10% make a great demand on the resources of a local church. They deserve help and ministry, without a doubt. However, counseling, as important as it is, leaves out the majority, the 90%, who still need discipleship...much of which occurs in the overall life of worship, word and witness in the local congregation. Yet, there is a significant number of church folks that do not need counseling, but at the same time struggle to get the most from the church and need assistance in their spiritual and natural life. Most Christians need coaching, all need discipleship and the place for all of this to occur is the local church, or the church of the locality.

Coaching, like counseling or discipleship, requires a set of disciplines and techniques designed to guide a person into new decisions and opportunities. Unlike counseling, this discipline is not looking for the negative effects of the past to overcome, nor is its spiritual formation alone, but a unique relationship designed to determine and enhance strengths to help someone reach their maximum potential in the Lord. Thus, once someone is equipped to coach (which hopefully you have already completed a coaching program), your skills will be of limited benefit if you do not let the world know that you are a coach on a mission!

This manual is a gift of our experience in developing a Coaching ministry for the local church. It is intended for those who have a similar sense of purpose and a vision from God to follow. It is designed to be informative, instructional, and inspirational. All the information contained herein is intended for your use as you develop your Coaching Ministry.

Stan E. DeKoven, Ph.D.

Acknowledgments

There are always so many people that deserve thanks when a project such as this is completed. I hope that I do not forget anyone who has helped me in this process.

First, I wish to thank my family for their continued support in my writing ministry, and my Vision International team that has stood with me these many years.

Most assuredly I wish to thank my wonderful friends who are marvelous coaches and even better friends, Bob Nolan, Dr. Tim Hamon, Dr. Sandy Kulkin and others who have coached and taught me much about the coaching practice, and how to take ones' gifts and utilize them for the Kingdom of God.

May the Lord receive glory, for this work is dedicated to His service.

Introduction

To those of you who read or purchase this book, it may not be necessary to discuss what I see as the essential need for Coaching ministry for the church. It may be like "preaching to the choir." Yet, I want to initially state some very basic tenets of faith regarding the ministry of Coaching as a discipleship program for the local church.

The church today is not really all that different than the religious community to which Jesus ministered when he came to earth. It was made up of people with different needs, problems, and life circumstances which affected their perceptions, motivations, beliefs, and behaviors. Jesus' ministry was spent primarily preaching, teaching, and healing those men and women who were the outcasts of the world (Mark 1:40). He continues to transform lives today.

There are important facts to remember about Jesus' ministry. Briefly, I will outline some here:

1. He was intimately involved with his world. Jesus deeply cared for the people to which He ministered. Even those who were totally unacceptable to the world were welcomed by Jesus (Mark 1:40). Coaching is designed to help men and women with untapped potential reach that potential for God's glory.

2. Jesus was not afraid to speak the truth in love. He pulled no punches with the woman at the well, yet he spoke with such compassion, authority, tremendous insight and wisdom. As coaches, if we are tuned to the Holy Spirit and trained to listen effectively, we too can teach others to speak and know the truth which will "set them free."

3. Jesus was well trained for the task placed before him (Luke

2:52). There is no excuse for any of us to be less than well prepared, academically or spiritually for the work to which God has called us. We must be instant in season and out of season, as we touch the lives of others.

4. Jesus was other-oriented, unselfish, and had a tremendous sense of timing. He knew when to confront, when to be silent, when to teach and when to touch. We as Christian Life Coaches must develop the "mind of Christ" in our response to the clients we serve.

5. Finally, Jesus was humbly submissive to his Father's authority. We must be willing to be in submission to the authority over us. Coaching is a valid, God-ordained ministry to and for the Body of Christ. Further, Coaching is an expression of love to those who are yet to believe.

As is often the case with any book, I am writing my introduction to this book after its completion. I use the word "completion" loosely, in that we see our Coaching ministry to be just beginning. Nevertheless, even though this manuscript is merely foundational, it is a necessary first step in the development of a coaching practice.

This book has been divided into five major sections. Section I describes the history, philosophy, program, and services which have proven to be highly effective forms of ministry in our local community. Every geographical area is different, and not all of the programs may be suitable for you. Each section can be taken and used as is or expanded to become program statements for public relations or ministry opportunities.

Section II, Policies and Procedures is an important section for those of you who feel called to direct your own Coaching ministry. Very few pastors/counselors are trained well in general administrative development, and it is important that your center operate in a smooth, administratively sound manner. This section will help you.

Public relations are so vitally important. Simply put, if the people to whom you want to minister do not know who, what, where, when, and about you, you'll never reach them. Public relations, which are discussed in detail in Section III, are a combination of planning and sales, mixed with prayer. This section may be the most important, as it will help you to develop a detailed plan of action for your ministry.

In Section IV, we continue with practical samples of public relations material that you are free to use. These helps will give you many ideas from which to grow.

Finally, Section V provides for you all the necessary administrative forms to be used to develop your Coaching ministry. We do not believe in "re-creating the wheel." Therefore, we have provided sample paperwork to assist you in creating your services.

This book has been a labor of love for its author. I pray that those of you who read and use this book will be blessed by it, and that many people to whom you minister will also be blessed.

SECTION I – History, Philosophy, Program, and Services

History and Models

Coaching as an Outreach Ministry

The goal for all of us as Christians is to become whole in Christ, to become all that he created us to be. He wants us to truly live out our lives as new creations, not constantly being buffeted about by the old nature. We are to truly live victoriously in Christ.

Therefore, we know that Coaching is part of the redemption process. Essentially it helps us to move a person in the direction of fulfilling their God ordained destiny in life. We come into agreement together in the Coaching process to see God move on behalf of the client.

Finally, the Coaching process is truly an integrative one; we integrate the best of psychology with the best of Biblical Studies realizing that the Bible is the absolute authority of truth, not psychological theory.

Therefore, the Coaching ministry is not just a "good idea" in the local church for people in the local church, but it is a tremendous opportunity for outreach ministry to those who hurt within our world.

A Discipleship Ministry

In the beginning of my Coaching ministry, I was unaware of the nuts and bolts of proper practice. My hope was to assist many individuals to solve problems, come to new insights, giving practical Christian solutions. For me, Coaching is a calling, not just a profession. It begins with a philosophy of ministry, which is provided here. Yours will be different, but you must be sure that your calling is pure.

Throughout this book you will see sections which say, *"Notes."* This simply means there are some specific insights that will help you to develop your practice in a more excellent way.

Statement of Faith

Note: A statement of faith or belief is one way for us to clearly distinguish ourselves as fellow Christians. People seeking help from a Christian professional will want to know of your faith in Christ. Here is a sample.

Tenets of Faith

We believe:

1. The Bible is the inspired written Word of God

2. The virgin birth

3. The Deity of Jesus Christ

4. The need for personal salvation through the atoning death and resurrection of Jesus Christ

5. The guidance of our life by the Holy Spirit through prayer

6. The return of the Savior

7. The establishment of the Kingdom of God on earth

8. Our call to minister to those in need and to facilitate healing of the same by God's grace.

Note: This, I acknowledge, is the basis for a doctrinal statement. In this type of ministry, we must always be of the attitude that Jesus expressed when he said, *"Whosoever will may come"*. All are welcome, and diversity of belief must be tolerated to be effective with those in need.

Where It Began--History

My coaching ministry began as a counseling outreach in early 1974, in San Diego, California. The dream of a Center for the Development of Personal, Family, and Spiritual Potential began with Dr. Joe Bohac and people of like vision. It started with a belief that the churches of America were and are to be the primary institution where all human and spiritual needs might be lovingly met. It (the church) was to be a living, healing community, where all people were welcome, regardless of race, creed, or dogma. It was to be the place where the "word might become flesh" and truly live with, in, and through those who believe. The church was originally designed for living, healing, and sharing common belief in Christ's provision for the Glory of God.

Over the years, the church in general has become institutionalized and liturgized to such an extent that people's needs were rarely met. It became unfashionable to believe that God could continue to "heal the brokenhearted and set the captive free." The church had become program oriented and social minded but lacked a true vision of ministry beyond its own inclusive walls. The restrictions placed upon the people of faith made it difficult to develop ministries with meaning designed to again restore the church as a living, vibrant community. It became essential to move beyond the church walls.

In the beginning, the major focus of ministry was to the beach community in San Diego. We began the Logos Coffee House and Counseling Ministry, Beach Outreach Programs, Logos Sounds, and our major ministry, the Logos House Ministries. The first few programs were transitory. Soon after encountering many runaway/throwaway children in the beach community, it was the decision of our leaders to begin the ministry of healing to young people through the group home concept. The Logos House Ministries provided quality Counseling services for troubled youth.

Simultaneously, Vision Bible College, under the leadership of Dr. Ken Chant, had begun in Australia. Vision International University, under the direction of Dr. Stan DeKoven, developed a coaching program to train men and women, and certify them through the International Association of Christian Coaching Professionals.

Coaching is a ministry with a definite vision. That vision is to assist and strengthen individuals and families to reach their potential in Christ, and, further, to strengthen the local church. Through the Coaching services, we attempt to help others become everything God intends a person to be, a process which coaching helps to discover. It is tremendous to see how free and responsible a person can be as he allows the Holy Spirit to control all aspects of his/her life. God can only use what we give to Him. We can only give Him what we know is there, our gifts, and our strengths.

Conclusion

We still believe that the Lord desires that His church be a discipling community to reach our generation for Himself. We are aware of the miracle of God's love for us, in that the Word (Logos) became flesh (John 1:1). His Word became flesh so that even though we were "yet sinners," isolated from God, lonely, scared, and depressed, He died for us (Romans 5:8). The Word, Jesus Christ, cannot be effective in our lives until His Word becomes intimately received by us. God desires that His people know Him intimately. He wants the Word to be the door through which we can reach our human and spiritual potential; and for the Word to be made known to the world through a Healing Community.

Note: Again, though briefly stated, it is important for you as the developer of a coaching ministry for your local church and community be able to articulate verbally and in writing why you are and what you are about. You may wish to use this as a model.

SECTION II – Policies and Procedures

Marketing Plan

The first essential in developing a good marketing plan is an understanding of the term. Marketing is often confused with sales, but it is distinctly different. Sales are the exchange of one's products (in our case "services") for an agreed sum of money or another valuable commodity. Marketing, on the other hand, has more to do with who is selling what, to whom, where, when and how. Marketing is that business activity involved with the advertising, packaging, and distribution of goods and services. A sound marketing plan will produce sales, but sales will never produce a marketing plan.

Through the years I have watched many ministries rise and fall. Some began on a "shoestring" while others spent thousands of dollars in advertising their services or product. Dollars do help of course, but they are not the whole answer to success. This is especially true in the 21st century, with the rise of the internet, webs, Facebook, etc. Social media marketing is here and now and becoming savvy of the usages and abuses of internet marketing is key for a coaching practice.

Fewer than one in eight new businesses in the United States survive the first year, and a business is not generally considered an "established practice" until it has survived for more than five years. The biggest cause of business failure is the lack of enough capital to properly fund the practice through its infancy. Underlying this cause, however, is usually the lack of a sound, manageable marketing plan. To develop such a plan requires sound answers to the issues raised above: the who, the what, to whom, where, when, and how aspects of selling your services to the consumer.

I say sell, even though some of you will be operating within church ministries that are wholly supported by contributions. We live in a fallen world, a world full of charlatans and a world full of cynics who have been "taken" more than a few times. Many portray themselves as ministers of the Gospel but have only larceny in their hearts. They are the wolves in sheep's clothing that devour the flock. To separate yourself from these carpetbaggers is essential, and to accomplish this, it is imperative that your ministry be what you say it is and does what you say it does.

The Who: Who Are You Selling?

Ultimately the One we desire to see lifted up and blessed is Jesus Christ but remember that you are His front-line ambassador. What are your talents and training? Are you a trained, experienced psychotherapist, a school psychologist, a certified substance abuse counselor, a marriage counselor or a certified temperament therapist? Telling the people precisely who you are, what you are, what you do, and by whose authority (i.e., Coaching under church exemption, registered therapist, etc.) is essential to establishing your credibility. Don't pretend to be what you are not, and never be ashamed of what you are. The Coaching ministry is a broad field, encompassing a breadth of knowledge that no one individual can encompass.

Sharing your personal testimony, or at least portions of it, in your marketing material, will help establish "who you are." Prospective clients instinctively shy away from coaches who have never been coached themselves and seek out those who "have been there" and can understand. The world abounds with single marriage counselors, childless family counselors, and "teetotaler" substance abuse counselors. We can learn to "incarnate" others' misery by placing ourselves in their situation and circumstance, as our Savior did, and effectively coach in areas we have no personal familiarity with; but probably never as effectively as when we coach in areas we have personally walked through. God's word says, "my strength is made perfect in weakness" (2 Corinthians 12:9), and

Paul further stated, "God chose the foolish things of the world to shame the wise men; and God chose the feeble things of the world to shame the mighty" (1 Corinthians 1:27 - Anchor).

We are most effective in our ministry when we coach in those areas where we have overcome something and have expertise, and where we have allowed the strength of God to do its perfect work. No doubt this is one reason that Jesus said, "Let me fully assure you, the man who has faith in me will perform the same works that I perform, in fact he will perform far greater than these..."

Think about the last time you heard someone tell their testimony. What impressed you: their native strength of character or the weaknesses they have overcome in Christ? Few people are impressed by a recital of our talents, and you will find this to be true of those seeking your help. They want to be understood, and as the axiom says, "Don't criticize another until you have walked a mile in his moccasins." Another thing about telling your story: your own testimony will help you recall the things you have experienced, - your thoughts and feelings of situations and events - and it will enable you to be an empathic listener and incarnational style coach.

The What: What Am I Going to Sell?

This may seem like a simplistic question requiring a simplistic answer, if any, but it is not. It is not enough to say, "I am going to provide 'Christian Life Coaching". Assessing your own strengths weaknesses, and limitations is essential to a good plan. What expertise do you have that can be used as a part of your coaching practice? For example, I have written in the areas of Marriage, Family and Parenting, and have significant expertise in these areas. Rather than counseling folks with significant deficits, I teach and coach best practices for good parents and for those with good marriages who want great ones. Thus, assess areas in your own life where prejudice could keep you from effective, empathic, incarnational style pastoral care to certain population groups, and work to ask the right questions to help someone grow in grace.

Recognizing your own limitations and staying within your own areas of expertise and experience will enhance your credibility. Never stop learning and expanding your areas of expertise and remember to keep your training ahead of your experience. Learning at your "client's expense" practicing beyond the limits of your expertise could be the most expensive lesson you ever learn.

Finally, remember that <u>what</u> you market must be something that fills a need in your community, or even your best effort will fail to sell your services. Knowing what your community needs is an important first step in developing the "what" of your marketing plan. It is true to some extent that with mass media advertising one can "create" a sense of need, but this artificial stimulus deals with product fads, and is rarely successful in selling services. In successfully selling services, it is imperative that you know what services your community needs, and who is presently attempting to meet this need. A carefully conducted community survey, or on-line survey via Facebook or other media will help you determine the needs of your community, which needs are being adequately met, and what you might provide to satisfy a service void.

To Whom: To Whom Am I Going to Make Sales?

Your community survey will also help you answer the next issue of marketing: "to whom" will you sell your services? Attempting to sell your services as an evangelical pastoral/counselor to the more liberal "mainline" segment of the church or to a predominantly Buddhist community will accomplish little.

Understanding your community, - its ethnic, cultural and spiritual make up - will enable you to tailor your product without compromising truth - to meet the makeup of your future clients.

A SAMPLE

On the next couple of pages is a sample questionnaire that you could use to survey the community you live in: You will also note some others later that can be very effective tools for your ministry development.

Coaching and The Local Church

Church Name:

Denomination:

Congregation Size:

Community Size:

Please indicate by number the five most critical personal and relational issues where people may need discipleship/coaching in your church and community:

Marriage and family life
Alcohol & drugs
Parenting
Communication
Unemployment or job enhancement
Christian Identity
Low self-worth
Business/stewardship
Spiritual growth
other (please specify):

Do you provide Coaching to your members?

- yes

- no

To your community

- yes

- no

Do you refer your members to others for Coaching?

- yes

- no

If so, do you prefer to refer to:

- Other pastors

- Christian Counselors

- Other

How many people request counsel or advice from you in an average month?

Of these, how many do you counsel?

How many do you refer to others _____

What is the average number of sessions you counsel with a person?

Do you find Coaching:

- a rewarding part of your ministry

- a necessity

Would you be open to a trained Christian Life Coach ministering to your members as an extension of your staff?

- yes

- no

Would you be interested in seeing some of your congregation trained in Christian "Peer" Coaching?

- yes

- no

Would you personally be interested in continuing your training in Coaching through continuing educational seminars?

- yes

- no

Would you be interested in your members, or yourself personally, participating in any of the following Coaching seminars conducted by Vision Coaching Group?

- yes

- no

Would you be interested in sponsoring one or more seminars in

- your church

- your community

- as an evangelistic outreach

If so, which ones

Would you support, through referral, a private Christian Coaching Clinic in your area?

- yes

- no

Additional comments, if any, you would care to make regarding Christian Coaching and its relationship to the local church. THANK YOU!

Where - Where Will You Sell Your Services?

The fact is, you can provide coaching services almost anywhere.... but eventually, you will want to work form a location that is professional and comfortable. Looking for the best location for a Coaching center involves more than finding the biggest office for the least cost. You may find a church that will offer space free, or at a very nominal amount, but in most cases locating your Coaching ministry in a church will limit your ministry to the members of the Body of Christ who share the philosophy of that church. This may not be a limiting factor in a large community, but in a smaller community it could spell disaster. We must recognize that there exists a high degree of parochialism within the body, and that being located within the physical facilities of one branch of the church (i.e., Pentecostal) may effectively limit your penetration of other segments of the Church.

Community surveys will usually give you a strong indication regarding the need for a Christian Coaching that is separate from any church- both in ownership and administration, as well as in the location of its physical facilities.

Determining where to locate your center is a marketing plan function known as "Site Selection," which considers several interactive factors. Look again at the people you have targeted to reach - the WHOM you desire to reach. Where do they live and where do they work? What is their general socioeconomic standing and their cultural values. Attempting to draw those of Oriental heritage, whose motivation is always to "save face," into an office located in a shopping mall are extremes of inappropriateness. Nevertheless, they demonstrate the need to select a site that is culturally sensitive to your targeted population groups.

Coaching is a sensitive issue to most people. To be sure there are those who take great pride in making known to all that they are regularly seeing a coach, and if God has called you to work with this group you need to be sensitive to their cultural norms (i.e., a plush office in one of the better professional centers where there is good exposure for them to be seen by their peers).

Transitional zones, between urban center and their surrounding residential areas often provide the most suitable locations for Coaching. Being out of the mainstream of the urban shopping areas they provide opportunities for more discrete clientele visits. Here you can often find a facility that offers the advantages of an urban setting (i.e., parking facilities, security patrol, etc.), yet preserves a bit of the more relaxing nature of a residential area. Be careful, however, to do your homework well before you sign a lease.

Check with the planning and zoning commission and building

department of your city or county. They can provide you with valuable information that will save you many hours in your search and perhaps hundreds of dollars in attorney fees trying to break a lease after you have found that the area you have located in is scheduled for urban renewal, is decreasing in population, or does not permit this type of business within the zoning code.

What other considerations are significant for you? Your own personal access to and from work needs consideration as well as other commitments you may have such as frequent visits to your church, proximity to your medical and psychological Coaches, supplier, etc. These may seem like small items, but over a period of a two to five-year lease they can add to or detract from your personal work enjoyment measurably.

If you offer early morning and/or evening appointments, the proximity of your office and residence could be critical. If you pastor a church in your area in addition to managing your Coaching center, proximity will again be a concern. There are, of course, no fixed solutions to these concerns as each of you may have a slightly different slate of concerns but do give them careful consideration.

Somewhere about this phase in the site selection process you will have to firm up your space requirements. Are you planning a one-man office, where a telephone answering service takes your calls, or will you be having a receptionist? Will you continue to work alone, or are you providing for growth and associates joining your ministry? Will you require space for your library and perhaps for your computer or word processor so that you can do other ministry tasks between appointments? Each of these require your careful and prayerful attention. The axiom that "haste makes waste" certainly holds true in office site selection.

You will invest a significant amount of capital for advertising, personalized stationary, cards, telephone listings, etc. And unnecessary relocations are not only costly in initial dollars expended, but cause shifts in your client base, as well as creating concerns among some as to your stability. Give yourself time to complete this step well. Then, you are ready to begin the search for your Coaching center's home.

Whether you do your own search or work through a realtor will depend a lot on the community and your personal knowledge of it and of the values of office space. If you aren't too sure of your knowledge in this area, I recommend using the services of a Realtor. A knowledgeable Realtor can save you hours and hours of looking and comparing. On the other hand, if you do feel comfortable in this field, go for it but don't be in a hurry to grab the first office that seems to meet your needs. Look at several and compare them against the criteria we have developed so far in this section. Rate them numerically according to how well they seem to meet your criteria. Then with this preliminary prioritization, go back and visit the owners of the various offices as well as the neighboring businesses.

Some owners will refuse to lease offices for a Coaching center, afraid of the kind of people it will attract. In other cases, you may find that one or more neighbors would strongly oppose your presence. Remember that you must live with your neighbors, even in business, and an undesirable relationship can be a source of constant aggravation. Eliminate these office complexes where owners or proprietors of established businesses do not welcome you. Honoring them in their wishes can result in one of the strongest bits of community public relations you will ever do.

When you have worked your way through the steps above, sit down and carefully evaluate the options left. Rate each option against each other and compare the cost to the individual site's rating. The best combinations or ratings - location and cost -need to be compared to site visibility, office exposure, handicap access provisions, etc. When you have done all of this, you have done the possible. Now take these to God and seek His wisdom; give Him the opportunity to do the impossible - to give you confidence in the selection of the most suitable site.

Finally, a suggestion in postscript. If you live in and intend to market over a large geographical area with low population densities, consider sharing an office with another professional - they face the same problem. This relationship allows the coach to use the facilities of the physician on those days he is in one of the other towns, thereby providing both professionals an office in three locations.

When – What Days and Hours will You Sell Your Service?

Now that you have determined where you will sell your services, the next question is when? When will depend somewhat on what type of Coaching you do. For instance, if you focus on marriage Coaching you will find that it is almost imperative to have some evening appointments. If you coach teens, then the hours right after school will be some of your busiest; and if you become involved in substance abuse Coaching (usually for relapse prevention) then the hours just before and just after work are the most critical. You may be tempted to try and cover all the bases - but a word of caution is in order.

Coaches, like others in ministry and the people-helping pro-fessions, are tempted to fall into the trap of workaholism and burnout. The need is so great and the laborers so few that it is easy to become rapidly over committed. You need to constantly remember that you will serve no one well if you are over committed, and no one at all if you push to the point of burnout.

How Will I Sell My Services?

While the Who, What, to Whom, Where and When of your marketing plan define the "out-working" of your ministry, the How is the in-working or "heart" of your plan. The "How" of a marketing plan will impact upon and modify' every other aspect of the plan. How you market your services will create the public's image of who you are and what you do. It will measurably influence to whom you will be able to provide service, and it will carry the message of where and when to your prospective clientele. The how involves the broad spectrum of your public relations material and your public relations plan.

It is imperative that you choose well the image you wish to present to your community and that you design your plan around that image. You may have unique skills and a vital ministry to offer to those in need. If you are to meet that need and penetrate your local market, you must not only have something to say, but you must - through your public relations material - say it well.

It is further recommended that you spend a couple of hours on Google, checking out various webpages and downloading interesting brochures, business cards, etc. that might work for you. Really, there is no need to reinvent the wheel…but it is essential that you develop solid public relations materials that have proven to be effective in portraying a positive professional image. Look them over and adapt them for your use, as you see fit. When you have developed a sample of the materials to convey your message, you must implement your plan. You will need to publish your public relations material, and you will need to develop a distribution plan. But first a word about printing.

Choosing a Printer

Having decided what you want to print, it is important that you find a quality printer who will do a professional job. When we developed our first brochure, we used a dear Christian man who printed ours for free. The price was right, but as the saying goes, "You get what you pay for." The quality of the work was poor, and we ended up waiting four weeks for something we had to throw away. Be sure your printer is highly recommended (check with friends) and avoid family if possible.

It is not necessary to spend a great deal of money on your public relations material. Just remember that what people see is the impression they will have of you. It may not change a bad counselor into a good one, but it will make a good one more accessible to the public you wish to serve.

Marketing: Direct or Indirect?

Marketing is usually comprised of two types: direct and indirect. Each has its place, and an understanding of the nature, benefit, and use of each is important in developing both your marketing and cash-flow plans.

Indirect Marketing

Indirect marketing refers to those methods of reaching unknown prospective clients with a general introductory message. Examples of indirect marketing are:

Facebook and Web pages are important; advertising on radio and T.V., in magazines, church bulletins, membership in referral services, etc. This type of marketing, in and of itself, produces few clients. It does, however, place your name before your prospective market on a regular basis. Inclusion of your business in direct marketing media also helps establish your image and adds to your credibility. The familiarity and credibility established in your prospective clients' minds through indirect marketing will pay big dividends, however, when coupled together with direct marketing approaches.

Media Ministry

Depending on the area in which you live and work, there may be opportunities for you to build your family Coaching ministry through the media. Through announcements of your Coaching ministry or workshops (Public Service Announcements) in the newspaper, an article or column, or through radio or television, people can be reached who want to hear from you. Creating Facebook ads for Free coaching services can be one of the most effective ways to move your practice forward.

Here in San Diego, I was a regular guest on a local Christian television program where we did a "theme" show on some problem in the Christian community. I have also been a semi-regular guest on two different major secular radio stations. There was no magic involved in getting onto these programs; we just asked. Radio, television, and newspaper people are always looking for someone who has something worthwhile to say, and if you can be creative, you might be able to expand your ministry through the media.

Your first step in establishing a media ministry is to find out what is presently available as resources. What is available for present programs? Is anyone presently offering advice on television, radio, or in print? Once you have determined (or created) the need, find out to whom you can talk and begin the process of establishing your media project. Take this person or persons to lunch. Be prepared to explore your ideas with them along with the needs of your community and how you might help them. Realize that you will be meeting with professionals, so do your homework. After listening to their needs and discussing some ideas, make a written proposal to them of your intent.

Be sure that you:

- pick up the tab for lunch
- send a follow-up thank you letter

After you have submitted your proposal, contact the station manager or editor to discuss things further. Even if they decline your offer, you have made a valuable contact. Stay in touch with these people periodically. Eventually, when they need an "expert' to address a community issue, you will be the first one they call.

A media ministry is not for everyone. You are clearly exposed to a certain amount of criticism, but the benefits may far outweigh the detrimental aspects.

Media marketing deserves some special consideration in your marketing plan.

Direct Marketing

Direct marketing methods include a broad range of activities undertaken to make direct contact with prospective clients and/or their families and friends. These methods will always produce more benefits than indirect marketing methods, but they are also the costly in time, finances, or both. Descriptions of some of the more common forms or direct marketing follow:

Key Referral List

Your best source of referrals for your ministry will be based upon the key contacts you make in your community. Enclosed is a form to use as a building block in the development of these friendships. (See Figure 1, page 85.) It is the foundation for your marketing endeavors and, therefore, is your key to success. How you contact the individuals on this list is up to you. However, I have listed below a general sequence of events that should prove useful for you:

1. Once you have developed your list, divide it into three categories: A, B, C. Section A would be your personal contacts with whom you already have a personal relationship, and whom you feel might be willing to help. Also, this would include people who would generally refer someone for Coaching services. If you are developing a non-profit organization, or are working through your local church, these people would be excellent recruits for either your Board of Directors or your Advisory Board.

   If you are a certified member of the International Association of Christian Coaching Professionals, you will have access to many men and women who are also actively pursuing coaching ministries and will be happy to help you with referrals in your area. Section B is a list of good potential contacts, but who are not presently involved in helping people. Section C is for all other potential referral sources but will not be as potentially helpful until you are more established.

2. After prioritizing your list, you will want to prepare a mail out or email letter which targets your referral contacts. If you have a local association of ministers, teachers, etc., and have access to their mailing-list, you may want to attempt a mass mailing campaign. Barring that, the effectiveness of a general mass mailing will hardly outweigh the energy output and cost. Instead, mail your public relations material with a personal letter to the individuals in Section A. The letter should be personal, professional, and must show a willingness to give away a service to this person or organization.

3. Five days after mailing these letters, you will want to follow-up with a phone call. Offer to answer any questions regarding your coaching services and to meet with them. If you must, offer them a breakfast or lunch, and be willing to pick up the tab. This is a small investment (and a deductible expense; save your receipts) for potential clientele. Be aware of good and bad meeting days (never mail on a Thursday as pastors are usually off on Monday), and be flexible.

4. At your meeting, be prepared to answer any questions that may come up. It is a good policy to try to get to know your contact better. Find out his or her needs; be a willing listener, don't give quick advice. Remember, your goal is to make a long-term, positive relationship.

5. Upon completion of your meeting, send him or her a nice thank you note. This should be personal, and it should focus in on the most important points of your conversation. Do not ask for referrals at this point but offer friendship. As you make follow-up contacts you can ask what you will from a friend. Do ask for other contacts that you could meet with their permission. Then repeat Steps 2-5.

6. When you receive your first referral from one of your

contacts, send them a thank you letter (See Appendix). At that point, you will want to offer them another lunch or breakfast. In all correspondence, be sure to enclose two or three business cards, just in case.

Direct Mail/Email

The second most successful marketing method we have used is email and direct mail. That is, sending a piece or pieces of literature to a generalized mailing list. This can be effective in:

1. Establishing visibility (the more your material runs across someone's desk, the more likely they are to remember you when it is time to refer);

2. Announce your arrival or something new.

When we first started, we were able to obtain a mailing list from a local Christian organization. We were so excited because we felt certain that our mailing would put us "on the map." After we went to the expense of having the printing done, stamping, bundling, and mailing.... we waited....and we waited. Later we found that most of the list was outdated and was made up of churches that were not particularly evangelical.

If, however, you can obtain a good mailing list (through such places as Youth for Christ, Young Life, Campus Crusade, local evangelical or church associations, etc.), it is possible to generate referrals. Make sure you enclose a response card for their convenience, but do not have great expectations. Unless you are the only Coach in town, pastors and other civic leaders get requests all the time. Remember, you must be willing to give away service if you are going to succeed in this ministry.

Workshops and Seminars

Another opportunity that you have as a professional coach is to teach others what you know. It has been my experience that people are looking for practical helps for life.

If you are going to develop a ministry that will effectively communicate God's love and bring in clientele for you to minister to, you must be willing to give something for nothing. The greatest something, we have, notwithstanding God's love, is ourselves and our expertise. The conducting of talks, workshops or seminars is of vital importance.

For some people, the thought of doing a workshop or speaking in front of a group is frightening. To lessen anxiety in that area, I attempt to speak somewhere, either a Kiwanis luncheon, church dedication, or in a workshop at least monthly. I have often felt as though I had little to say, but with good preparation and practice, most people can speak to small groups. Groups are generally grateful for a free speaker and will remember if you did a good job. Make sure you leave plenty of business cards and fliers - that's expected.

The development of a workshop or seminar is a much more difficult task. It takes special planning and coordination. It is a lot of hard work if you try to do it alone. Most of the workshops we do are co-sponsored by area churches or schools, which have the people power to help develop the program and defray the costs. If possible, offer to ride on the coat tails of the church or school and just help support their efforts. The more visible you are, the more likely you are to receive referrals. In the beginning, we would teach Sunday School Programs on various topics just to get more comfortable with speaking. Every contact you make can pay dividends down the road. Remember, the more you give the more you receive.

Professional Relationships

Professional relationships developed with other coaches, counselors, physicians, psychologists, psychiatrists, chiropractors, etc. will both add to your professional image and generate clientele. Counselors, psychologists and psychiatrists often encounter counselees whose problems are outside their personal experience, and sometimes we all experience personality conflict. It is important for them to have developed relationships with peers to whom they can refer these cases.

Physicians and chiropractors frequently see patients whose principle problem is neither biological nor structural, but more focused on goals and dreams yet to be accomplished. They will often be willing to refer a client to you as coaching and not counseling or medical intervention is needed.

Pastoral Referrals

You will want to contact the pastors and other religious leaders of your community. Your expertise can help them lighten their load, enhancing their own ministry. Be sure to advise them that as a Christian Life Coach, you are in a support ministry to help the local church, rather than to supplant it. You will find most will welcome you, support you, and become one of your best referral sources.

Client Referrals

Your own clients, grateful for the wonderful coaching you have provided, will be the best source of referrals. Give them a small supply of our public relations materials, i.e., fliers, brochures, business cards, etc. and encourage them to pass them around among their friends and family. You might even consider giving your clients a free session when they refer a new client that signs up for a series of Coaching sessions with you. And remember, since your successful coachees will always be the most believable references, make sure that what they have to say is good. Treat them right and your ministry will flourish.

Funding Your Marketing Plan

First and foremost, remember that marketing doesn't cost, - it pays. Without a marketing plan, the sales you make will be incidental, if not accidental. An old axiom applies well here: "It is unwise to pay too much, but it is far worse to pay too little." Should you pay too much, you will lose a bit of cash, but if you pay too little you lose the cash as well as the benefit of an unusable product.

Marketing cost will vary, particularly in start-up. Your market area and targeted population groups will, to some extent, dictate the type of public relations materials developed. Your geographical area and the unique demographics will impact your use of various media. After start-up, however, marketing programs have a lot of commonalty. To maintain a good marketing effort in a limited geographical area for professional services, you should devote approximately five to eight percent of your gross revenues. This amount should, if used wisely, cover the costs of both direct and indirect marketing - including business cards, brochures, flyers (which are sometimes categorized as supplies), web, Facebook, etc.

Marketing is not an easy task, but it is an essential part of being in business - even the business of Christian Ministry - if you are to succeed. If you have a clear vision, a systematic marketing plan, and attainable goals in implementing the plan, then the only limitations are those placed upon yourself. Your own creativity, or lack thereof, and your personal motivation are the only limits to successful marketing.

SECTION III – Planning

Developing Your Plan for Ministry

Pre-Opening Procedure

In retrospect, there are several pre-opening questions that you must ask yourself before you ever sign a lease or send a letter. Take some time to read the questions and formulate some responses in as much detail as you can. The answers to these questions will assist you in the development of your Plan for Ministry Development and will become a checklist for action and review. Before reading on, take a few minutes to work through this questionnaire. Don't avoid it! Procrastination will kill your ministry before anything else. You must be like the five wise virgins: have plenty of oil to keep your light shining bright.

Plans for Ministry Development

Take a moment to look over your answers. Have you left anything out? Have you allowed yourself to "dream dreams?" At any time, you can add or delete items from your think sheet. You should keep this questionnaire as a personal historical document. It is always exciting to look back after three to six months of work to see from where you have come, how your plans have changed, etc. Remember, a plan is only a guide to be submitted to the Holy Spirit for approval and guidance. It is not an iron clad Magna Carta!

PLAN FOR MINISTRY DEVELOPMENT
(See Figure 2, page 86.)

Fill in this form candidly. It is your next step towards meeting your goals.

Vision - What is my vision for ministry:

Gifts/Talents - What do I have to offer to my world that makes me unique?

Limitations - What limitations do I have, and how can I overcome them?

Population - Who do I want to serve? Why?

Now that you have brainstormed by answering your questionnaire, it's time to begin to translate this into a "vision." This is where the hard work really begins. If I would have done a better job of pre-planning, we might have had fewer rough spots during the early development of our ministry.

Again, using our Plan for Ministry Development form. begin to translate your ideas (from the questionnaire) onto the areas listed. This may take much more time to do, and you may want to solicit the help of a trusted friend or family member. Bouncing ideas off someone can assist you in crystallizing your thoughts on paper. Once you have completed this process to your satisfaction, you will be ready to then design your Plan of Action.

Plan of Action

You have now answered most of the very difficult questions facing you. You are beginning to see what your coaching ministry will look like. Now it is time to develop your Plan of Action. This will serve as the blueprint for your work. This form, along with your personalized resource list, will become very important over the next few weeks and months. You must become very familiar with the Plan of Action if you are to implement it successfully. Remember, as you begin to reach out into your community, you will encounter many open doors and many closed doors. Prayer should precede any change in your vision, but we must be flexible enough to hear God's voice. Be willing to modify your plans as new opportunities for ministry become available.

Plan for Ministry Development

(The answers shown are examples.) (See Figure 3, page 87.)

Fill in this form candidly. It is your next step towards meeting your goals.

Vision - What is my vision for ministry:

> *Develop a coaching ministry for local churches around the world to effectively minister to the body of Christ*

Gifts/Talents - What do I have to offer to my world that makes me unique? *Excellent communication, visionary and writing skills. I have the educational and ministerial background to develop the work that God has called me to.*

Limitations - What limitations do I have, and how can I overcome them? *Sometimes I push people too hard. I need more love and patience. I need finances and personnel help. Will ask parents for a loan.*

Population - Who do I want to serve? Why?

> *The Churches of America and Internationally, as the Lord*

opens doors, because of the need to treat and coach others.

Calling - Why me, Lord?

Why not me? With God's help, the work will be done.

Cost - What risks do I take? Am I willing to "weigh the cost?" *Possible rejection of Coaching idea. Lack of control of who runs the project*

Instructions: This form is not to be taken lightly. If used properly, it will take you one step closer to meeting your ministerial goals.

Statement of Purpose - In your own words, where do you want to go? Write this as though you were going to propose this to your family, friends, and associates (eventually you will).

Sample: Develop a national coaching ministry.

Target Population - In terms of type, income, geographical location, race, religion, etc., who will I try and reach? Narrow your vision, you can always expand later.

Sample: The church and community.

Long-Term Goal - Where do you want to be when you are 83? What are your 25, 15, 10, and 5-year plans? Be specific. Put feet to your prayer.

Sample:

5-year plan – clients in all 50 states

10-year plan – Train multiple coaches to assist me

15-year plan - Turn over to someone else to run

25-year plan - Start the next career

Short-Term Goal - What do I have to do tomorrow and work up from there. Keep it simple.

Sample: Complete the editing, publishing of this manual.

Public Relations Steps - Who do I contact first? Next? etc. How will I do so? Personally, by phone, by letter?

Develop marketing strategy

Advertise in magazines and by direct mail

Re-Evaluation - Every three to six months I must re-evaluate my direction.

How? Coach, friend? To what extent?

Pre-Opening Procedure Questionnaire (See Figure 4, page 88.)

Answer the following questions as honestly as you can.

1. I would like to start a Coaching ministry because...

   a. *God has called me*

   b. *I like people*

   c. *I hear that coaches are liked by everyone (here!)*

   d. *Coaches make big bucks!*

2. My training and experience to do this work include...

   a. *Degrees*

   b. *My experience*

   c. *Good experience as client*

3. It is time for me to make a change. I want to change...

   a. *My job*

   b. *My health*

   c. *My income*

   d. *My life*

   e. *My wife, etc.*

4. Economically, I want/need/deserve....

    a. Nothing

    b. $100,000 per year

    c. Etc.

5. I feel called by God to this ministry because...

    a. I have always been a helper

    b. Everyone likes me

    c. I need to help others

    d. God spoke to me through a burning bush

6. If I had unlimited resources, I would...

    a. Travel the world

    b. Quit my job and coach full time

    c. Do nothing different

7. My family supports me/does not support me in my Coaching effort because...

    a. They think Coaching is taking too much time from family

    b. Very supportive of all my work

8. I have 20 hours of time per week to devote to my ministry.

9. I am prepared to invest $1,000 and 20 hours of time to make this ministry go.

10. My best abilities lie in areas of...

    a. Communication

    b. Loving people

    c. Writing P.R. material

11. My biggest problems are...

    a. Money

    b. Not enough training

    c. Lack of confidence and fear of failure

12. How I could make my ministry fail...

    a. Never begin

    b. Not plan well

    c. Never ask for help

13. How I can make my ministry a success

    a. Prayer

    b. Hard work

    c. More training

You will notice that there are six major sections in your Plan of Action. In Section V, P.R. Steps, you will want to list any person, program, church, etc., who might be able to help you in the development of your ministry. This contact list will be made up from the Key Person List.

It is very important that you make a clear plan of contacting these people on a systematic basis. You will be amazed to see how many people are willing to help if you are willing to humble yourself and ask. At this point, take some time to complete Figures 3 and 4 in the back of this book, this is ok! When you have done so, you will have a working document from which to develop your ministry.

Follow Through

Unless you have a clear vision, of how to develop a ministry (or a plan to reduce your deficiencies) and have a plan for the development of your ministry with the necessary contacts to help you, you are not yet ready to begin. Before embarking on any endeavor, you must be willing to weigh the cost, and take a risk. Even with the best of information and help, a new adventure is always somewhat frightening. When we opened our first office in

Pacific Beach, California, we were terrified, and that's a good sign. There is only one way that your ministry will succeed, and that is if you completely trust in the Lord (Proverbs 3:5-6). The road ahead is paved with obstacles, but if you truly desire to develop a ministry to people who are troubled, lost and dying inside, then GO FOR IT! With God's help, a lot of perspiration, and a good plan, all things are possible.

SECTION IV – Public Relations

Marketing Your Ministry

During this past year, I have watched the rise and fall of many ministries. Some have spent thousands and millions of dollars in advertising their work. We deal with a cynical world, and justifiably so. There are many who will portray themselves as ministers of the Gospel who have only larceny in their hearts. It is vital that your ministry be what it says it is and do what it says it does. In other words, we must have integrity.

One of the most frequent questions in the beginning was, "How can we get more bang for the buck? How can we let people know that we are available to minister to those in need?" Over the past 11 years of ministry, we have had cost and time commitments. Some of the ideas are not our own, however, were inspired by two books you may want to obtain: Private Practice Handbook and How to Build a Practice Clientele Using Key Referral Sources: A Source book, by Charles H. Browning, Ph.D. Ordering information for these fine books is available in the bibliography of this manual. The key referral list is one of the four primary tools used for ministry development, and the most effective. The other three are Direct Mail Marketing, Workshop and Seminar Development, and Using the Media. All are used with a basic philosophy that you cannot out give God. The more you give away in service to your community for the Lord, the more God will release His blessings from His storehouse for you.

Developing Your Public Relations Material

It is important that you choose the image you want to present to your community carefully. You have unique skills and a vital ministry to those in need. If you are going to reach out to your world, you must not only have something to say, but you must say it well in your public relations material.

Coaching Possibilities

To follow are some specific programs that might be implementable in your community…these are but a few examples of ways you can promote and develop your coaching practice.

Church Assistance Programs

We offer to the San Diego Community and beyond comprehensive coaching for the family. Specifically, programs include:

1. Coaching Services for the whole family.

2. Workshop development, promotion and presentation for preventive help.

3. Seminars in Family Ministry.

4. Consulting Services to local churches.

5. Other ministries which are supportable by our staff and professional services division.

Note: We have found that you must do much more than just 'hang out a shingle' if you are going to effectively minister to your community. In our years of full-time Coaching practice, we have gone from 0 to over 300 clients per week; from one small office to six Family Care Centers. We will further discuss the advantages of direct mail, but the use of these outreach programs is the ministry of our community development ministry.

Program Components

Each Christian Life Coach who desires to create or enhance their Coaching ministry will want to provide services to the community which are unique to meet needs. When we began our Coaching ministry, we started with the contacts and expertise we had. Our primary experience had been Coaching Christian youth. We therefore started our services by contacting pastors and youth leaders that might refer people to us. The program components listed here are an outgrowth of the unique needs of our community. You will want to survey your area and design services to meet the hurting souls in your world, based upon your gifts and calling. These program statements are samples of what you can do but are certainly not all inclusive.

There are three divisions of our Coaching and educational ministry. * They are described as follows:

I.   PROFESSIONAL SERVICES

"...for the development of personal and family potential."

It is extremely important that you state as clearly and succinctly as possible what your specific purpose is. This is an example. We give this to clients, pastors, etc. to know "where we are coming from."

General Information

The Center's Purpose

The Center was established for the express purpose of providing educational and Coaching services and consultation from a Christian perspective to individuals, groups, families, and churches. In doing so, we endeavor to help those with whom we come in contact to reach their spiritual potential. It is our belief that if we, as God's people, can remove the weight of sin that so easily besets us," we can become all that God created us to be.

There are many blocks to our reaching our potential in Christ. Burdens of the past, fear of the present or the future, unresolved guilt, and inappropriate life decisions are but a few. Family Care

Center was formed to help the people of God to resolve, remove, and move forward in developing healthy relationships with God and man. We are pleased to have the honor of ministering to you, and we trust that God will guide both of us as we move toward the development of our spiritual potential.

What to Expect

You have come to the Center seeking assistance. This is an important first step and could be a significant turning point in your life. There are three vital things you can do to help yourself and your counselor. They are:

1. During your first session or two, you will be encouraged to fully tell your story to your coach. It is important that you be open and honest with your feelings. This can be difficult at first, but we will be with you to help in the process. Though your problem is truly unique, you are not alone. You will be given a DISC profile and other assessment tools to help us in the process of communication and planning.

2. You did not, in most cases, develop the difficulties you are now experiencing overnight. Just as it took time to develop, it will take time to solve. Each problem is different, and it is important that you plan to stay with the coaching process until it is completed. The ultimate responsibility for your getting well is yours and God's. Your coach is a facilitator of your growth.

3. During your coaching, you will receive assignments of "Homework' which will help speed up the change process. Such assignments as reading God's Word or Christian literature, even writing assignments may be given. The more involved and cooperative you are, the sooner the process can successfully end.

We are aware of the difficulties of living in our present age. It is our prayer that we can serve you and assist in helping you to better handle life's difficulties in the love and grace of God.

Coaching Services

Note: This material is a brief program statement that can be utilized for promotion to local pastors and other referral sources. Further, we used this information in our major Coaching brochure. Though a brochure is not essential, it is quite helpful in letting people know about you and your work. See the section "Sample Letters & Etc.' for sample brochures.

What is the purpose of Christian Life Coaching?

We are dedicated to serving people in the process of wholeness. We believe that man is a Tripartite being (Spirit, Soul and Body), and that it is intended for all people to be whole. Yet, so many people are unable to reach their personal potential.

Some people can handle life's situations alone, however, there are times when it can be helpful to share these issues with an accepting, professional coach. It has been noted that "peace of mind does not come from the absence of problems and difficulties, but the ability to cope with them."

Our purpose is to provide loving, caring, professional assistance to people in the development of their personal and spiritual potential.

What services does the Coach offer?

We specialize in:

- Individual, Group assessment
- Coaching for effective Child and Adolescent development
- Marriage Conflict Coaching
- Substance Abuse Coaching
- Stress Reduction

- Seminars and Workshops
- Coach Services

Location

The main office of the Center is in San Diego, California.

Office Hours

Office hours are from 9:00 a.m. to 5:00 p.m., Monday through Friday. Evening and weekend appointments are available by appointment only. Our receptionist will have a staff member contact you at the first opportunity.

Fees

The Center is a ministry of Vision International Education Services, Inc., a non-profit, non-denominational, Christian organization. It operates on fees charged to clients and through private contributions. All fees are based on a sliding scale according to family size and income. No one will be refused services for financial reasons.

The Staff

Professional Coaching services are provided by a certified Christian Life Coach.

Stan E. DeKoven, Ph.D., founder and director, is a licensed Marriage, Family, and Child Counselor, and a Certified School Psychologist. He received his Ph.D. from the Professional School of Psychological Studies in Counseling Psychology. He also graduated from San Diego State University and was awarded his Master of Arts Degree from Webster University. Dr. DeKoven is a certified Substance Abuse counselor and is certified as a Christian Life and Executive Business Coach through the Institute for Motivational Living.

Note: In most states, a licensed minister, or someone with a certificate in Christian Life Coaching can be a coach. As of this writing, there is no specific licensure required for someone to practice coaching.

Note: In addition to our general Coaching program, we have determined some specific needs of our local community. When you find a need and fill it, you create an opportunity for ministry. These are examples of the many outreach programs which can be effective for you.

Coaching and the Church

As a church grows, the need for family life ministry in the church will increase. When you talk about family ministry, you are not talking about family counseling, or formal coaching for that matter. However, both counseling and coaching can be excellent additions to a local church programs and services.

What you are specifically addressing is the need to provide for the educational, social and spiritual needs of all members of the family regardless of their time and position within the life cycle. That is, ministry services must be developed which are designed to meet the needs of all age groups.

Most local churches have several programs that are already actively ministering in certain areas. For instance, some may have Awana programs for children, Children's Church, Worship Center, and home fellowships, all of which impact the family positively.

There is a need for special ministry services designed to assist families to become more of what God intended them to be. Family ministry is ministry to families that are struggling through issues in their lives, and to train and hopefully prevent families from disintegrating even further.

As we all know, the family is in trouble in our society. There has been a significant breakdown of traditional family patterns and moral standards. Approximately every five years a family moves from one part of the country to another, leaving an absence of the normal family roots with which they became acquainted in times past. We live in a culture that values rugged individualism versus community and family. This has caused family breakups, domestic violence, child abuse, etc. These types of problems are now at an all-time high.

Further, there are people who have physical and financial needs which must be met. It is the responsibility of the local church to have impact into our community, and to address to the best of their ability, and in keeping with the church's vision, these pressing needs.

There are many other areas that can be dealt with in a family ministry program. These include: marriage enrichment programs, family Coaching services, training in basic parenting, adolescent issues, drug and alcohol abuse, etc.

Sample Proposal

Along with the section above, you would want to put together a proposal for the church to provide coaching ministry to the family. What this proposal is designed to do, is to present to the Board (or elders, deacons, etc.) a proposed ministry program for the local church, designed for implementation over a period of time, under the supervision of the Board and Pastoral staff. It is important to review this with an open mind and heart, prayerfully seeking God's guidance in this, looking not only at present needs, but at future needs which will obviously come because of the growth of the local church.

What Is Family Ministry?

It would be easier to say what family ministry is not. This information is given to you from an excellent book by Royce Money, Ministering to Families: A Positive Plan of Action. Mr. Money gives eight primary things that it is not, then I will share with you what family ministry is.

1. Family ministry is not simply a building or a facility,

although ministering to the family certainly does occur within a facility most of the time.

2. Family ministry is not merely a catalog of church or community programs, it is only a part of the effort.

3. Family ministry is not another appendage to a continually growing church program like evangelism and missions. Family ministry must be integrated into every aspect of the church.

4. Family ministry is not just a passing fad, nor is it just an American phenomenon, it is a necessary part of the body of Christ since we are all members of a community of believers.

5. Family ministry is not just for nuclear families, that is, mom, dad, and children. It is relevant for the entire body of Christ.

6. Family ministry is not just for church families, it is one of the finest outreach tools that we have available to us. Every time we reach out to touch the life of someone in our community, assisting them to meet a need vital to their lives, we extend the Gospel.

7. As stated above, family ministry is not merely a Coaching service. For some families that type of specialized individual group or family Coaching is necessary, but that is for a minority of the church. For the most part, it is a positive enrichment and growth-oriented teaching and training aspect of the local church.

8. Family ministry doesn't have to be expensive. Great expenditures of money are not needed for a church to minister to its families. This will be addressed later within this proposal.

A family ministry is a focused ministry attempting to prevent and enrich the members of the local church. It is designed to assist families to become more whole and integrated within their world.

This is needed because of the tremendous changes within our society, the isolation that families experience because of the mobility of our world, and the need to have a sense of belonging in the local church. This ministry is vital especially in Urban areas because of the recreational aspects of life that draw family members away from one another and because family members tend to be rather insecure. We live in a very insecure world. We have just come out of what we call the "me" generation. These insecurities can affect marriages, families, and all aspects of family life.

Also, family ministry is to address the loneliness issues of people's lives. There is a need for intimate relationships now more than ever before. Our media and all aspects of our society attempt to push people toward fragmentation. Family ministry is designed to assist people to stay focused on the needs of their own families and give them the tools necessary to meet those needs.

Finally, families tend to be rather ill equipped. I am often amazed at how ignorant people really are (this is not a put down, **it** is just an observation) about handling the basic issues of life. Areas of financial management, child rearing, marriage communication, sexual issues within marriage, how to handle teenagers, are all issues that are addressed within the context of a family ministry.

Assessing Family Needs*

It will be necessary for you to clearly assess the needs of families within your local congregation. Remember that while the needs may not be great at this point, you must assume that the needs will increase the larger the church becomes. Therefore, **it** is essential that you do some sort of an assessment. Attached to the back of this proposal is a copy of an assessment tool that could be used within the home groups to determine whether there are valid needs within the church. This is certainly not a fully scientific instrument, but **it** will help in planning future ministry.

In summary, the family needs that we will attempt to address include:

- The need for Christ to be the Lord of each home. God created the family to bring glory to Himself through Christ. We see that in Psalm 145:4-7.

- Family members need love for one another because it is only through love that the family can survive the many trials of life (1 Cor. 13:7, Eph. 5:25).

- Parents have a primary responsibility of teaching their children to love and obey God. God has given parents the responsibility of educating their children. This is not to be delegated lightly (Deut. 6:4-9).

- Children are to honor their parents because God commands and rewards such respect (Eph. 6:1-2).

- Family members need to feel secure in their homes because the threat of harm destroys love, trust and harmony in the family (Col. 3:19-2 1).

- Who does the family need? They need God, they need the Word, they need the pastoral staff, they need the body of Christ. You need to have a focused ministry that will address the needs of families once you determine fully what those needs are.

SECTION V – Administration Forms

Policies and Procedures

For any organization to function, it must have a basic structure. Of course, if you are solo practitioner, you will need little more than a business licenses and some basic bookkeeping. If you desire to grow more as an organization, you will need a structure to work from.

In this chapter we will look at our basic organizational structure. Whether or not you have your own non-profit organization or would like to establish your ministry as a for profit or LLC, it will help you to more clearly delineate your own organizational structure.

For those interested in establishing a Coaching practice in their area, in cooperation with the International Association of Christian Coaching Professionals, there are two options. One being a general affiliation organizationally (if you have your own nonprofit) or as an established Center, under our charter We can assist you in becoming legally incorporated to function as a Coaching ministry.

If you are interested in becoming a ministry of IACCP, please complete our request for an Affiliation Agreement. The benefits of affiliation include discounts on testing materials, books and podcasts, as well as available consultation in ministry develop-ment, public relations support, and much more. We would be happy to give you further information (see 2, Application for Affiliation, in the rear of this book).

For Profit or Non-Profit?

One of the first decisions that must be made in developing a Coaching ministry is should I be for profit or not-for-profit? I would strongly recommend you consult with a well-versed Christian C.P.A. or Administrative Coach who can assist you in your decision. It has been our experience that a properly established non-profit corporation provides the best covering, structure and flexibility for you in which to develop your ministry. Listed in the back of this book under "Resources' is a ministry that can help you in this process.

Ministry Policies

In the rest of this chapter I have provided a sample of some essential policies you will need to establish for your protection and professional development. Not all potential policies are provided, just some of the more essential ones.

Money Matters

First, let me categorically state, money matters. You need it, you want it, and you can make it as a Christian Life Coach. It is the love of money, not money itself, that is the root of all kinds of evil. Money is simply a tool, a necessary one, and essential in coaching practice. Remember the concept of implied value. If something is free (or too low cost) it is not worth anything. Thus, whether you are for profit or nonprofit you must have profit...or your work will not be profitable to anyone.

As a non-profit ministry, we have a policy that we never turn anyone away for a lack of money. As we have given our service away, the Lord has blessed us even more. Occasionally someone will take advantage of our fee policy, but generally those clients who cannot pay much become the greatest supporters.

For example, I had two clients that were unable to pay but the bare minimum (at the time) for their Coaching, however, they felt so good about their personal and professional growth that they have referred over 20 full paying clients in one year! God is faithful as we trust Him.

Giving away service as one of the primary ways of building your ministry will be discussed further in the section on Public Relations.

Sample Sliding Scale

(Recommended)

Gross Income	Fee
$25,000 or less	$50.00
$29,000-31,999	$60.00
$32,000-34,999	$70.00
$35,000-37,999	$80.00
$38,000-40,999	$85.00
$41,000-43,999	$90.00
$44,000-46,999	$95.00
$47,000-49,999	$100.00
$50,000 and up	$150.00

Note: As I have mentioned previously, not all clients can pay much, yet almost all can pay some. I have even made a contractual commitment for Christian clients to read God's Word and pray for our ministry on a regular basis (good coaching by itself).), and for non-Christians to attend a local church. You are limited only by your imagination.

Getting Them Started

When a client calls, it is vitally important that they feel accepted, that they are heard, and that they feel a sense that you care and can help. Your Intake Procedures need to be conducted in a professional manner, and the essential information regarding the client must be obtained.

All materials received must be kept confidential. You should always keep copies of your Intake Forms to use them for future planning, for public relations purposes, and to find other referral sources. This will be discussed in more detail in Chapter 5.

Intake Procedures

It is the intention of any coaching ministry to be as fair and equitable as possible in providing clients to its associates. We want all our staff to be successful and well compensated. Our intake procedure is simple and straightforward. The steps are listed below:

1. All intakes should be handled by a Director or designated representative. Basic information is gathered on a prospective client on a phone intake form and the client is assigned a therapist based upon the following criteria:

   A. Client need and preference (i.e., if the client needs or requests a female vs. a male therapist);

   B. How client generation occurred. (If generated by a personal referral, the client will go directly to the therapist who generated the referral);

   C. If from general advertising, we look at:

      1) geographic location

      2) therapist availability and scheduling.

2. If there are any questions about this procedure, please contact a Director for clarification.

Note: As the Lord allows, part of the vision of our coaching ministry is to establish a National and International network of Christian Coaching affiliates. We hope to eventually advertise this in appropriate ways, utilizing an 800 number so that we may refer clients to our affiliated centers via phone, computer and fax. More on this as it develops.

Client Record

Keeping a case record on each client can be a tedious task. However, it is vital for your own professional growth and for your personal protection.

All client records must be kept safe and reasonably up to date. Your notes should include the date and type of services provided, a summary of your discussion and a statement of your feelings about the client.

Case Record

Beginning with the Intake Interview, a case file should be created. In each client file there should be at minimum:

1. Completed intake forms to include payment information;

2. An initial history of needs and your impression;

3. A running process note for each client hour with date of service and summary of your session.

The client records need to be kept fully confidential.

Telephone Procedures

The office phone is for business only. It is to be used for business-related matters, i.e., scheduling clients, collateral contacts, public relations, etc. Calls of a personal nature (other than to your home, and then only brief calls are allowable) which do not pertain to business will be charged to the individual Associate. We attempt to keep our overhead as low as possible to allow us to see a wider variety of clients. This is our commitment to ministry.

Note: Good stewardship dictates that you keep your overhead as low as possible. When we began our ministry, we started with a small but comfortable office that had a common receptionist, a conference room (for meetings and groups), at a very low cost. In any ministry, you must weigh the cost of the venture.

PERSONAL NOTE

I have worked for many years with a vision of developing a ministry that will assist people in their growth and development. We are proud and honored to be a part of this ministry. It is by no means perfect, but it is emerging as a force in the bringing forth of God's Kingdom.

We are only beginning. It is a privilege to have each Associate on staff. We are grateful for God's riches and blessings. It is our hope that you too might fulfill a vision of helping people become all God created them to be.

In this section we have provided some basic sample forms, contracts, and letters that will help you get things started. None of these are original but are a synthesis of forms that we have found to be useful. As you review them, you will find a need to modify them. However, I feel the basic forms you will need are clearly provided here.

It is our philosophy to keep our paperwork to a minimum. We feel we have done so by requiring the few forms which follow. We covet your suggestions and comments on any changes that might help. Also, for minimal cost we can provide all the forms found in this book on computer disk for your modification and usage.

Coach Contract/Agreement

A consulting Agreement by _____ and between: _____ hereinafter referred to as CLIENT; and XYZ COACHING, hereinafter referred to as COACH.

DEFINITIONS:

1. Coach: Person or Organization providing professional services under a contractual arrangement and serving as a private contractor.

2. Client: The recipient of said contractual services provided by said Coach under the provision of this contract, as hereinafter set forth.

TERMS AND CONDITIONS:

1. The Coach acknowledges that he/she is a private Contractor or professional Coach. As such, he/she shall provide services to The Client, according to goal specific directives. Specific directives may include but are not limited to Coaching clients for alcohol and/or chemical substance dependence, crisis Coaching, etc., according to established protocol.

2. Coach understands that as a private contractor he/she assumes all responsibility for his/her actions and forever holds harmless the client, its successors, assignees, designees, and devises.

3. Coach understands that as a private contractor he/she is responsible for all federal state, and local taxes on his income, as applied by law.

4. Coach shall procure and maintain in force, liability insurance with limits of not less than $200,000.00 for student level counselor, and not less than $500,000.00 for

professional Coaching. A copy of said policy shall be furnished to the Client upon request.

5. It is agreed and understood by the Coach that he/she will not knowingly diagnose any medical condition or biologically induced psycho pathological condition, or psycho/social pathology behavior. When same may be suspected, the counselee will be referred to the appropriate professional.

6. Clients, who after evaluation by the appropriate medical or psychological Coach, may be found to benefit by a multiple disciplinary (Holistic) approach, the Coach, may in cooperation with clients primary medical or psychological care giver, provide Coaching services.

7. Coach's primary office is Coach's individual responsibility. Other meeting arrangements can be made between the client and the coach at both party's agreement.

8. Coach will be remunerated for services on a per session basis in accordance with Schedule A attached.

TERMINATION CLAUSE:

This contract shall be binding in full force until revoked by either of the parties by written agreement, providing the other party not less than thirty-day notice. Executed by the above-named parties on the date hereinafter shown:

Coach_____Date_____

Client _____Date_____

Witness: _____Date_____

Dated this_____day of _____in the year _____of Our Lord.

I understand that my coach will help me understand myself, assist me in clarifying my goals, and help me look at alternative solutions to achieve my goals. I further understand that I am fully responsible for the decisions I make concerning my life and behavior. I understand that the Coaching modality is one of "wholeness," designed to help me focus on achieving optimum wholeness, personhood and health, encouraging me to seek and find an enriching, fulfilling life.

I further understand that I am responsible for payment of all Coaching services provided for me or for my minor child, if applicable. I clearly understand and agree that all services rendered to me are my personal financial responsibility. I also understand that should I suspend or terminate my coaching, any fees for services rendered me will be immediately due and payable.

Client:

_____Date_____

Guardian:

_____Date_____

Client Assessment

Client Name:

Date of Intake: Emergency?

Address:

City: State: Zip Code:

Patient phone number:

Employer:

Parent (if patient is a minor.):

Patient's primary care Physician:

Name:

Address:

City: State: Zip Code

Phone number

Evaluation requested by:

Location of Evaluation:

Identifying Information: (Age, marital status, nationality, sex, education, occupation, etc.)

Presenting Concern and goals of Coaching:

Family History: (Birth order, brief family of origin history; summary of past and present relationships; economic status that might affect the coaching process.

Dating, Courtship and Marital History for relationship coaching:

Education: (Dates and degrees; school performance (grades); difficulties and discipline problems; sports and other extra-curricular activities; highest grade completed; area of study)

Occupation: (Employment history; status; job satisfaction; present financial status; unemployment or underemployment; welfare or S.S.I. benefit history; job related problems; military service - branch of service, type of discharge, dates and discipline problems)

Mental Health Background: (Past treatment, hospitalization or medications, past episodes, family history of emotional problems)

Substance Abuse History: (For Substance Abuse coaching, to include past treatment, substances used in past/present, date of first use of all substances, substances of preference, history of abuse including dates/times of last use and frequency of use for each substance, occurrences of overdose, withdrawal or adverse drug reactions, problems due to drug use including date problem first occurred and date of last occurrence, family attitude toward us as a child, and now.

Client Rights Statement

PRIVACY OF CLIENT INFORMATION: I understand that all information to the agency will be treated with the utmost confidentiality. Coaching Centers will release information concerning a client only under the following legal conditions:

1. with written consent of the client

2. by order of a court of competent jurisdiction

3. in cases of child abuse or molestation

4. to prevent homicide or suicide

Records remain the property of the coach who shall retain sole authority to determine specific information to be released and the suitability of any potential recipient.

Cancellation Policy and Financial Responsibility: I understand that I am responsible to keep my coaching appointments, and that I am to notify the office 24 hours in advance of any appointments which cannot be kept. If I provide less than 24 hours' notice, I will pay one-half (1/2) the fee charged for my usual appointment.

Clients Rights Statement: I understand that as a client of XYZ Coaching, I have:

1. The right to confidential treatment of my personal records as outlined in the Privacy of Client Information statement above.

2. The right to professional coaching by appropriately qualified coach.

3. The right to appropriate contact with supervisors or administrative personnel to discuss difficulties with the coaching staff or policies. If such contact does not resolve the situation under discussion, I may request a meeting with the Coaching Director (if there is one).

4. The right to have my fees for coaching adjusted when there

is a change in my income.

5. The right to refuse procedures offered or prescribed by the coach at my own discretion.

I acknowledge that <u>I have read and received a personal copy</u> of this statement and have had the opportunity to have any questions about its contents answered in a satisfactory manner.

Client_____ Date_____

Coach_____ Date_____

Contract for Change

<u>1. What do I want to change that would enhance my life?</u>

<u>2. What would I need to do in my life to make this change?</u>

<u>3. What am I willing to do?</u>

<u>4. How will others know I have changed?</u>

<u>Client_____</u>

<u>Coach_____</u>

Coaching Session Record

<u>Client:</u>

Session #

Primary Goals:

Evaluation of Last Week's Homework:

Session Notes:

Date:

Time:

Fee:

Homework Assignment:

Agenda:

Christian Life Coaching Servicers

IRS # _____

Bill of Services

For: _____

Client Name: _____

Referring Physician: _____

Date of Service	Place	Procedure	Detail	Charges

Total   Amount   Current

Due Paid Balance _____

Signature of Coach: _____

Date: _____

Plan for Coaching Ministry Development

Fill in this form candidly. It is your next step towards meeting your goals. **Vision - What is my vision for my coaching ministry:**

Gifts/Talents - What do I have to offer to my world that makes me unique?

Limitations - What limitations do I have, and how can I overcome them?

Population - Who do I want to serve? Why?

Your Information for Clients Brochure

Information for My Clients

Welcome to my practice! I appreciate your trust and the opportunity to be of help to you.

Because coaching includes clarifying, I believe we will work most productively and comfortably together when we are most unambiguous with each other.

This letter is designed to answer some frequently asked questions about my practice and our relationship, so please read all of it before you sign it at the end. As you read it, please feel free to mark any places which are not clear to you or write in any questions which come to your mind, so we can discuss them at our next meeting. This brochure is yours to keep and refer to later.

I ask that you read and sign this information brochure to indicate your understanding of office procedures and your willingness to abide by these policies.

1. Coaching as a profession

You can only make the best decisions if you have enough information and understanding of how this coaching process works. Let me discuss some aspects of coaching as I see it.

My Coaching approach is aimed at insight that leads to action...new decisions based upon new and better information.

Coaching is a large commitment of time, money, and energy and so a Coach should be carefully chosen. I strongly believe you should be comfortable, encouraged, and optimistic with the coach you choose.

Coaching is not like visiting a medical doctor, in that it requires your very active involvement and efforts to change your thoughts, feelings and behaviors. I will ask for your feedback and views on your coaching, the efforts and progress we are making, and other aspects; and I will expect you to be open about these. Offering your views and responses when they are important to you, even if I don't ask, is one of the ways you are an active partner in your coaching. You will have work to do both in the coaching hours and many times during the day. Change is not instant, painless, or passive; there are no "magic pills." Instead, there will be home-work assignments, exercises, practice sessions, and perhaps other projects. Probably you will have to work on relationships and make long-term efforts. Change will sometimes be easy and swift, but more often it will be slow and frustrating with a need for repetition.

So that we know exactly where we are going, I will ask for regular reviews of our progress and if coaching is not progressing, I cannot ethically just keep working with you. I may then suggest that you see another coach or professional in addition to me. I will fully discuss my reasoning and recommendations with you ahead of time so that we can come to an agreement.

I take an essentially educative approach to people's problems and so encourage you to learn more about the kind of coaching I do. I would like you to become knowledgeable about its goals, methods, effectiveness so that you will be able to use it without me.

I see coaching as a collaboration between two adults, one who defines the problem areas to be worked on and the other, who (as a Coach with specialized knowledge), helps in making the desired change. By the end of the first or second session I will be able to offer you my initial impressions and a verbal plan (which will change somewhat as we progress). I will tell you what I think and feel about your situation. You will then be able to make the best decisions, in your own best interest.

If we are to work together, we will need to specify the goals, focus and methods of coaching, the approximate time commitment involved, costs and other aspects of your situation. Before going further, I expect us to agree on a plan to which we will both strive to adhere to. Periodically, together, we will evaluate our progress and goals and, if necessary, redesign our coaching plan, goals and methods.

As with any powerful process, there are both benefits, and risks associated with coaching. Risks might include experiencing uncomfortable levels of feelings like sadness, guilt, anxiety, anger, frustration, loneliness, and helplessness; recalling unpleasant aspects of your history; or appearance of being judged.

Despite this, you should know that coaching has been repeatedly scientifically demonstrated to be of benefit for most people and in most situations. Relationships and skills may improve dramatically. You may be better able to cope with social, career or family relationships, and so receive more satisfaction from them. You may better understand your personal goals and values and thus grow as a person and become more mature.

I do not take on clients whom, in my professional opinion, I cannot help using the techniques I have available. I will, therefore, enter our relationship with optimism and an eagerness to work with you.

2. Scheduling

I usually schedule 1 and 1/2 hours for the first introduction and information-gathering session and then meet at about weekly intervals for one half or one hour each time. We will schedule our meetings cooperatively for our mutual convenience. I will inform you of my vacations or any other reasons I may not be in the office at least one month ahead of time. Feel free to ask about my schedule in making your own plans. Since I do brief coaching, typically we will meet for three or four months and then less often over several more months.

An appointment is a commitment to our work and a contract between us - we each agree and promise to be here and on time. On occasion, I may not be able to start on time. For this I ask your understanding and assure you that you will receive the full time agreed to. If you are late, we will probably be unable to meet for the full time scheduled, as it is likely that I have another appointment scheduled after yours.

Your session time is reserved for you. Reality does not always allow us to keep our promises, but a canceled appointment is an interruption in our work which will delay completing it. I am rarely able to fill a canceled hour unless I have a week's notice. I will make our meetings a priority and ask you to do the same to keep missed hours to a minimum. If they exceed one every three months or so, I will have to charge you for the lost time unless I am able to fill it (your insurance will not cover this charge).

I do not have available personnel to supervise your children in the reception room while we are meeting. Therefore, I request that you do not bring children with you if they are so young as to require supervision. I do provide reading materials suitable for older children, but we do not provide toys.

3. Fees

In any professional relationship, payment for services is an important issue. This is even more true in coaching, where clarity of relationships and responsibilities is one goal of coaching. You are responsible for assuring that services are paid for; this demonstrates your seriousness, sincerity and maturity. My current regular fee for coaching for everyone is $150 per session. In unusual circumstances we may, before the end of our first meeting, negotiate other arrangements. Because this is a substantial commitment of money, although certainly not out of line with similar professional services, it requires that we work efficiently and energetically. I will assume that our agreed-upon financial relationship will continue in effect if I provide services or until you inform me, in person, by telephone or by certified mail, that you wish to end it. I will expect you to pay for any services rendered to you until the time you terminate the relationship.

4. Billing and payments

I would greatly prefer that you pay each session at the time of our meeting, or in advance for a series of sessions. Please do not interpret this as any distrust of you or lack of faith in your responsibility and maturity. In my personal coaching, I have found that this arrangement kept our attention focused on our goals and so was most productive. It also allows me to keep my fees as low as possible because it reduces bookkeeping costs. May I suggest that you make out your check before each session begins so that our time will be used most productively.

At approximately six-week intervals I will send you a statement indicating, cumulatively, all our meetings and the charges for each; and, when you have paid off your account, I will send you a final statement for your tax records. If we have agreed that I bill you, I ask that you pay me within the next five days for the services I have already rendered to you. There will be a re-billing fee of $5.00 to cover the expenses of supplies, preparation and postage on accounts overdue by 30 days or more.

If there is any problem with my charges or billing, or any other point, please bring it to my attention and I will do the same with you. Such problems can interfere greatly with our work and must be resolved openly and without delay.

5. Contacting me

Out of consideration I usually do not take calls when I am with a client; I will note the call and, as soon as I can, pick up the message you have left on my voice mail.

I cannot always be reached by phone immediately; but if you leave a message, I will get it the next morning. Generally, messages will be picked up and calls returned daily except on weekends and holidays. I have found, in most cases, that telephone Coaching is very effective, as is Skype or Facetime.

6. Confidentiality

I regard the information you share with me with the greatest respect, so I want us to be as clear as possible about how it will be handled. In general, I will tell no one what you tell me. The privacy and confidentiality of our conversations, and my records, is a privilege of yours and is legally protected by federal and state law and by my profession's ethical principles, in all but a few rare circumstances.

Because, in my case, I am a mandated reporter, and even though the likelihood of our discussion on these personal matters is low, I must share this with you.

There are two other situations in which I must, by law, tell others some things you might tell me: when I believe you intend to harm yourself or another person and when I believe a child (or elder) has been or will be abused or neglected. If you have concerns about confidentiality, please raise them with me so that we may resolve them and proceed with our work together.

Otherwise, I do not and will not tell anyone anything about our coaching, or even that you are a client, without your full knowledge and usually a signed Release of Information Form. If this is of concern to you, ask for a blank copy of my Release Form to review. Further, I promise to send out nothing without your full approval even to your physician or the professional who referred you to me.

7. My way of doing coaching

Each coach has been taught and has expanded upon a way of doing coaching. He or she has developed rules or methods which have worked well. I will be happy to explain or clarify these if you would like more information.

I often lend books, which you may keep if they are of use to you; but I ask you to return them so that I may lend them to another client. I may also give you photocopies of articles or informational handouts which are yours to keep.

I often take notes and ask my clients to take notes, both during the session and at home. If you record our meetings, you can review at your leisure the points we covered. I will, in addition, negotiate homework assignments with you. These are a crucial component of personal change and I expect them to be completed fully.

I may want to make audio records of our sessions to assist me in the coaching process. I now ask your permission to do this and assure you that nothing more than is necessary to understand your situation will be shared with a colleague and that he or she is legally and ethically pledged to respect your privacy and confidentiality as am I. You can refuse this recording or insist that the record be edited. I promise to destroy this recording as soon as it is no longer useful to me for my consultation or, at the latest, when I destroy your case records.

8. Your case records

You have the right to review your records in my files at any time, to make additions or corrections and to obtain copies (only with your written permission, of course) for other professionals to use.

9. Termination

Termination is inevitable. It should not be done casually, as it can be made a most valuable part of our work. Either of us may terminate our work if we believe it is in your best interest. I ask that we meet for at least one session after you wish to terminate to review our work together, our goals and accomplishments, any future work to be done, and our options. If you would like to take a vacation from coaching to try it on your own, we must discuss this, but we can often arrange it to be productive.

10. Evaluation of our coaching experience

If at any time, you feel dissatisfaction with any aspect of coaching, please discuss your views, reasons, concerns or plans or whatever is troubling you with me as soon as you can, so we can resolve the problem.

Besides our regular reviews of progress during coaching, as part of my responsibilities as a professional I will send to you, about six months after our last session, an evaluation questionnaire. I ask that you agree, as part of entering coaching with me, to return this follow-up form.

11. Contact person

If, during our work together there is an emergency, or I become concerned about your personal safety or the possibility of your injuring someone else, I am morally and legally obliged to contact this person:

Name:

Address:

Phone: Relationship to you:

Because we all need to know we are in good hands, I indicate my credentials below. If you wish more information on my background or training, please feel free to ask. I am a Professional coach, a licensed Marriage and Family Therapist, and a certified substance abuse counselor, and have been in coaching and counseling practice for over 40 years.

- Doctoral degree in Counseling Psychology form the Professional School of Psychological Studies, 1983.

- Licensed as a Marriage and Family Therapist in California since 1980

- Member of the American Association of Marriage and Family Therapists

- Also, a Certified Forensic Counselor, Substance Abuse Counselor, and member of several other professional associations.

12. Complaint procedures

If you are dissatisfied with any aspect of our work, please raise your concerns with me immediately. Dissatisfactions will make our working together slower and more difficult if not resolved.

13. Additional points

By the way, although I share this office setting with other professionals, each of us operates independently and is solely responsible for the quality of the care he or she provides.

In my professional practices, as therapist, Coach and teacher, I do not discriminate in accepting and treating patients, clients, students or others on any of these bases: age, gender, marital status, race, color, religious beliefs or creed, belief, ancestry, national or ethnic origin, ethnicity, location of residence, physical or mental disability or handicap, veteran status, sexual orientation, health status, having a criminal record unrelated to present danger-ousness, or in violation of federal, state or local laws or executive orders. This is both a personal commitment and is made in accordance with federal, state and local laws and regulations. If you believe you have been discriminated against, please bring this matter to my attention immediately.

14. Agreement

I, the coach, having interacted for a suitable period, find no reason to believe that this client is not fully competent to give full consent to the coaching process, and will benefit from the process. Furthermore, believing this client fully understands the issues raised above because I have personally informed the client of the above-stated issues and points, discussed them, and responded to all questions raised, I agree to enter coaching with this client as is indicated by my signature here:

Today's date: /   /20

I have read (or had read to me) the issues and points stated above, discussed them where I was not clear about those points, had my questions fully answered, and understood and agree to comply with them, I hereby agree to enter coaching with this therapist as indicated by my signature here:

Today's date: /   /20

Please return a signed copy of this agreement to me and I will give you a copy to keep for yourself.

I truly appreciate the opportunity you have given me to be of professional service to you and am eager to receive your questions, comments, suggestions, or concerns at any time. I look forward to a successful and beneficial relationship with you. If, as we proceed, you are fully satisfied with my services, I, as with any professional, would appreciate your referring other people to me who might also benefit from my services.

Agreement to Pay for Professional Services

I, the undersigned, request that the above-named therapist provide professional services to me/or _____
as a client, and I agree to pay this coaches fee of $ per for these services.

I have read this coach's INFORMATION FOR CLIENTS brochure and agree to cooperate with and abide by all its provisions as indicated by my signature there.

If the client is a minor, I understand that while I have a right to general information on issues and progress, some information shared in this professional relationship will be held in confidence by the coach and the minor child.

If, at any time, I am dissatisfied with this coaching I will fully discuss my views, reasons and plans with the coach (and if the client is a minor, with the client named above).

I agree that this financial relationship will continue in effect with the above named professional if this coach provides services or until I inform him or her, in person, by telephone or by certified mail, that I wish to end it. I agree to pay for services rendered to this client up until the time I terminate the relationship.

I understand that I am responsible for charges for services provided by this coach to this client, although other persons may make payments on this client's account.

Signature: _____

Printed name: _____

Relationship to the patient: _____ Self _____ Other: _____

Date: /   /20

Home address:

Figure 1 Referral List

Referral List			
Contact	Email	Address	Phone

Figure 2 Plan for Ministry Development

Vision - What is my vision for ministry:

Gifts/Talents - What do I have to offer to my world that makes me unique?

Limitations - What limitations do I have, and how can I overcome them?

Population - Who do I want to serve? Why?

Figure 3 Plan for Ministry Development

(The answers shown are examples)

Fill in this form candidly. It is your next step towards meeting your goals.

Vision - What is my vision for ministry:

> *Develop a coaching ministry for local churches around the world to effectively minister to the body of Christ*

Gifts/Talents - What do I have to offer to my world that makes me unique? *Excellent communication, visionary and writing skills. I have the educational and ministerial background to develop the work that God has called me to.*

Limitations - What limitations do I have, and how can I overcome them? *Sometimes I push people too hard. I need more love and patience. I need finances and personnel help. Will ask parents for a loan.*

Population - Who do I want to serve? Why?

> *The Churches of America and Internationally, as the Lord opens doors, because of the need to treat and coach others.*

Calling - Why me, Lord?

> *Why not me? With God's help, the work will be done.*

Cost - What risks do I take? Am I willing to "weigh the cost?" *Possible rejection of Coaching idea. Lack of control of who runs the project*

Instructions: This form is not to be taken lightly. If used properly, it will take you one step closer to meeting your ministerial goals.

Figure 4 Pre-Opening Procedure Questionnaire

Answer the following questions as honestly as you can.

1. I would like to start a Coaching ministry because...

    a. God has called me

    b. I like people

    c. I hear that coaches are liked by everyone (here!)

    d. Coaches make big bucks!

2. My training and experience to do this work include...

    a. Degrees

    b. My experience

    c. Good experience as client

3. It is time for me to make a change. I want to change...

    a. My job

    b. My health

    c. My income

    d. My life

    e. My wife, etc.

4. Economically, I want/need/deserve....

    a. Nothing

    b. $100,000 per year

    c. Etc.

5. I feel called by God to this ministry because...

    a. I have always been a helper

    b. Everyone likes me

    c. I need to help others

    d. God spoke to me through a burning bush

6. If I had unlimited resources, I would...

    a. Travel the world

    b. Quit my job and coach full time

    c. Do nothing different

7. My family supports me/does not support me in my Coaching effort because...

    a. They think Coaching is taking too much time from family

    b. Very supportive of all my work

8. I have 20 hours of time per week to devote to my ministry.

9. I am prepared to invest $1,000 and 20 hours of time to make this ministry go.

10. My best abilities lie in areas of...

    a. Communication

    b. Loving people

    c. Writing P.R. material

11. My biggest problems are...

    a. Money

    b. Not enough training

    c. Lack of confidence and fear of failure

12. How I could make my ministry fail...

    a. Never begin

    b. Not plan well

   c. *Never ask for help*

13. How I can make my ministry a success

   a. *Prayer*

   b. *Hard work*

   c. *More training*

About the Author

Dr. Stan DeKoven is the International President of Vision International University[1], and founder/President of the Vision International Training and Education Network.[2] Vision/VITEN specializes in establishing and supporting local, Church-based Bible Colleges and distance education programs. Through their unique "Bible College in a Box" system, they are presently serving more than 4,000 Resource Centers in over 150 countries and over 100,000 students through its affiliated ministries.

Stan has a diverse background in Education, Business, Military, Leadership, and Counseling. He has pioneered two very successful businesses while consulting with others nationally and internationally. Stan has earned a bachelor's degree in Psychology from San Diego State University, a master's degree in Counseling from Webster University, a Doctor of Ministry degree from Evangelical Theological Seminary and a Doctor of Philosophy in Counseling Psychology from the Professional School of Psychological Studies. Dr. DeKoven holds credentials in School Psychology, Marriage and Family Therapy, and clinical membership in many professional organizations.

He specializes in Leadership development, and assisting executives achieve their potential in the marketplace. He is also an Executive

---

[1] Vision International University (www.vision.edu) is a California State Degree granting Institution, primarily offering their programs on line or direct distance (correspondence) and Church based programs. Vision has offered Associate-Doctorate, in Theology, Leadership, Counseling and Christian Education since 1989.

[2] The International Training and Education Network offers practical training in religious studies through the International Training College in over 140 nations, and in multiple languages, publishes Christian literature in multiple languages, and certifies ministers and counselors for service in and through the local church.

Coaching Specialist for The Vision Group, and the founder of Walk in Wisdom media ministries.

He is a licensed Marriage and Family Therapist in the State of California with over 35 years of professional services, specializing in:

- Crisis Ministry
- Domestic Violence and Recovery
- Substance Abuse Treatment
- General Family problems with children and Teens
- Personal Coaching for men and women seeking improvement in vocation or relationship

Books by Dr. DeKoven

- *Crisis Counseling*
- *Family Violence: Patterns of Destruction*
- *Substance Abuse Therapy*
- *Kingdom Quest: The Journey to Wholeness*
- *New Beginnings: A Sure Foundation*
- *Marriage and Family Life*
- *On Belay! An Introduction to Christian Counseling*
- *Group Dynamics*
- *I Want to Be Like You, Dad: Breaking Free and Discovering the Father's Heart*
- *Grief Relief*
- *Parenting on Purpose*
- *Old & New Testament Surveys*
- *Fresh Manna (How to Study the Bible)*
- *Leadership in the Church: In the Eye of the Storm*
- *Visionary Leadership*
- *Prelude to a Requiem: Principles of Leadership from the Upper Room*
- *Supernatural Architecture (The Apostolic Church of 21st Century & Beyond)*
- And 20+ more books and booklets in various topics, see at www.booksbyvision.org

Dr Stan speaks on a wide range of topics from Christian Business, Christian Counseling, Leadership, Team Dynamics, Personal Coaching, Church Consultancy, Setting up Local Church Counseling, Teaching and Mission Ministries, World & Urban Missions, Youth, Church Structure and Personal and Corporate Vision.

Dr Stan assists many younger ministers develop in ministry. Through speaking and consulting, he gives relational oversight to churches both nationally and internationally. As such, he is in demand around the globe to speak in Leadership Conferences and to teach in Bible Colleges/Universities.

To schedule speaking or contact the author:

Vision International University: www.vision.edu
Walk in Wisdom Ministries: www.drstandekoven.com
Or call 760-789-4700

Additional Resources

- *A Leader's Life Purpose Workbook: Calling and Destiny Discovery Tools for Christian Life Coaching* by Tony Stoltzfus

- *Christian Coaching, Second Edition: Helping Others Turn Potential into Reality* by Gary Collins

- *Christian Life Coaching Handbook: Calling and Destiny Discovery Tools for Christian Life Coaching* by Tony Stoltzfus

- *Comprehensive Christian Coach Handbook, Second Edition: Essential Guide to Spirit-Led Coaching and Business Success* by Leelo Bush PhD

- *How To Hear God: Keys To Hearing God's Voice Every Day (Christian Life Coaching Guide Book 1)* by Lynne Lee

- *Leadership Coaching: The Disciplines, Skills and Heart of a Christian Coach* by Tony Stoltzfus

- *The Coaching Mindset: 8 Ways to Think Like a Coach* by Chad W. Hall

- *The COACH Model for Christian Leaders: Powerful Leadership Skills to Solve Problems, Reach Goals, and Develop Others* by Keith E. Webb and Gary R. Collins

www.ingramcontent.com/pod-product-compliance
Lightning Source LLC
Chambersburg PA
CBHW061458040426
42450CB00008B/1409